To: Rich.

My friend.
Brother & fellow
Traveller on the Aerospace
highway...
Enjoy!

Randy -2016-

The Story of Randy Turnbow and His Aerospace Company

Joshua 24:15

The First 50 Years of E.M.E., Inc.

The Story of Randy Turnbow
and His Aerospace Company

Dedication

This book is dedicated to Randy Turnbow:
A man that simultaneously grew a company and a family,
A man that instilled both Christian faith and values,
A man that is loved by many because he has given much.

Acknowledgments

Author:
Art Stricklin

Editors:
Brenda Turnbow
Michelle Turnbow
Melissa Hammonds
Wesley Turnbow

Table of Contents

CHAPTER 1

The Turnbow Standard: Family First

What is the strength behind EME plating and metal finishing? The answer, says EME Chairman Randy Turnbow, "We have these two unshakeable bonds—faith and family. That has been a big portion of the reason for our success." Randy purchased the company in 1972 and has become the family patriarch. Faith and family are the foundation of EME's good name in the competitive metal finishing business in Southern California. This family-run company has been together for more than five decades, serving each other and their customers.

Aerospace metal finishing involves applying hard, impervious coatings to metal in order to enhance or protect a particular part of an airplane, helicopter, rocket, or satellite. It is this adding of layers which helps strengthen and improve an unprotected piece of metal so that it is able to withstand extreme pressure and intense stress during critical points in its life. For decades, this is exactly what the Turnbow family has done for each other, their employees and their customers; applying layers of hard work, love and commitment, especially during tough times, to create a solid work environment, impervious to any difficulty that comes their way. And one does not build a company from the ground up without difficulty.

"Over the last 50 years EME has been in business, we have had nearly every kind of employee problem, legal battle, financial struggle, equipment failure, customer loss and management fights possible," Randy said. "But through it all, the Turnbows have loved and cared for each other in a way I could never express. With God's continued blessing, we will still be very successful many years from now, and hopefully one or more of our grandchildren will be involved to continue the tradition of good character and honorable service that we have brought to the aerospace metal finishing industry."

Layer by layer, coating by coating, year by year, day by day, the Turnbow family has added strong faith, good character, and undying support to each other's lives and the lives of hundreds of employees, customers and friends. They have worked together, lived together, laughed, and prayed together, even fought together. They have been there for each other in those times of extreme pressure and intense stress, during the most critical points in their lives. They have strengthened these unbreakable bonds of faith and family to withstand the test of time. Proof of this is in the longevity of their family-owned company.

The summer of 2012 marks the 50th Anniversary of EME, Inc., in Compton, California. It is a milestone rightly celebrated, but this milestone is not the end. In typical EME fashion, it is the intent of the company to use this success as a launching pad, continuing to focus on doing well for each other, their customers, and their employees.

Because of this focus, today, EME has 15 employees who have spent more than 20 years at the company. For many of them, it is the only job they have ever known. Another 15 employees have spent 15 or more years in these humble buildings, near where Randy and his brother Steve, the current President of EME, grew up. "Sometimes we will have employees leave here and when they come back they'll say that other companies are not like EME. "Other companies don't do it this way," said Quality Control Manager John Lopez, Sr., a 28-year EME employee.

The family's foundation began to be laid in the early 1930s, not on the aerospace floors of Southern California, but on the iron horse of the railroad; the mechanical beast which roared into California from Utah, carrying 16-year-old Lee Turnbow, the future father of Randy and Steve.

Lee had been raised in the "Beehive State", but moved to the "Golden State" of California, alone, to carve out a new way of life. His step-father, Walter Hamilton, was the first of the Turnbow clan to find work in the aerospace industry. He served in the World War I Army Air Corps near Long Beach, California, where he settled and later worked at North American Aviation. Walter introduced Lee to the trade of airplane machining not long after Lee left the dry-cleaning business trade.

Lee never advanced past high school in formal schooling, but he carried a brilliance that astounded those around him. It was Lee who laid the Turnbow foundation, which is still rock solid today. "I couldn't wait to see what Lee was doing next when I came to the plant," said Dalton Turnbow, Randy's middle son. "He had a true engineer's mentality and could fix anything." "We always said there was nothing Lee couldn't build with a piece of 2-inch pipe and a welder," Wesley Turnbow, the current CEO added.

Hardened by the Great Depression, Lee Turnbow always had a variety of jobs, including working as a machinist at Screw Products Corporation of America. But ultimately the most important job he worked on was with California Metal Processing in 1954, because that is where he would hone his skills in aerospace metal finishing.

Evelyne Turnbow had arrived from Kansas by automobile at age 15 and cared little about the metal plating business at first, but was soon drawn to the brilliant, driven, future aerospace engineer who was planting himself firmly in the still-growing California aerospace business. She first met Lee, and later married him, while she was working in her family dry-cleaning business. "Lee was just a brilliant man. All he did was go to high school, but he never stopped reading and learning; he even made his own plans for our house which we built in Ojai,

California. His plans were accepted, without changes, the first time they were submitted to the city planning office," Evelyne proudly said.

Lee is the one who started the idea of the family all working together. While Lee never piled up loads of material riches, he poured his life and his street-honed skills into his family and others. "Our beloved dad was the genius, that's what people called him. 'The Genius,'" said Steve Turnbow. "And because he was a man of the Great Depression, Dad saved anything and most everything he found. He could make just about anything we needed from the stuff he found for free. Seriously, though, he was truly a mechanical genius. I'm truly amazed by my old man, the Genius from the Great Depression. He's the toughest man I ever met." Lee brought great assets to the new young company. He could work on boilers used for heating the tanks. He could work on the rectifiers that supplied electric DC current for the plating and anodizing operations. He could design and build a crane to lift the work, and build an entire building which he did as required.

For a while even Evelyne worked in an aero-space machine shop in Gardena before Lee thought it was time to start training up the next generation of Turnbow men for leadership. That meant it was time for Randy to enter the business. He had already been working in the aerospace industry as a machinist in high school. At Lee's insistence, Randy enrolled in the Magnaflux Corporation School of Non-Destructive Testing (NDT). There he graduated as the youngest certified inspector in their history, at the age of 17.

Because of his Depression upbringing, Lee was convinced that the way for any young person to be prepared in the post-World War II world was to have two professions, so that if the economy turned sour, he would always have something else to fall back on. That turned out to be just what Randy did. He attended college at nearby California State University in Long Beach and also was a 2nd Lieutenant in the California National Guard. But during the same time he worked part-time as a machinist and sometimes metal finisher. Randy began to realize that he had a real interest in the metal finishing, finding it both creative and challenging. This fascination would provide the avenue for spending the rest of his life working in aerospace industry.

Randy inspected aerospace parts all through the time he was in college and for two years after he got out. "I will forever be grateful to my dad for making me get a second job because I always had something I could fall back on. I had worked at a company named California Metal Processing every summer almost from the beginning, and I worked there as an inspector during my senior year of high school," Randy continued. "I always liked the trade. It's a never-ending, demanding job, but is something I really enjoy."

The area where Randy grew up was perfect for a young man with ambition and a desire for success in the aerospace industry. In the 1960s, Southern California was undoubtedly the largest aerospace manufacturing center in the world. "Everybody was here when I was growing up. Lockheed had a plant, Hughes, Rocketdyne, Bell Helicopter, General Dynamics, and Rohr all had plants here; as well as Northrop and Douglas, and North American Aviation, which were headquartered here. Even now, if you combine the Los Angeles and Orange County areas, it's still the largest aerospace manufacturing and processing hub anywhere."

It turned out to be the prime area for a young man and his father to discover the aerospace industry and live their dream. "Lee started working with parts from the DC-3, then the DC-8, even as Douglas Aircraft became McDonald Douglas Aircraft and then finally, the Boeing Co. He worked with them all," Evelyne said.

But Randy had already found his most important discovery during junior high school. He had met his future wife, Brenda, who attended nearby Bixby Knolls Christian Church. There they met when a friend invited him to a Christian Youth Fellowship group that was meeting there. Although Randy and Brenda dated all through high school, they had to be reunited in college while Brenda was attending Chapman University.

Brenda soon knew enough about Randy to be very interested in him, however, she knew very little about the aerospace finishing industry. "I knew Randy worked in the summer for his dad in the shop, but that's all I knew. At first I felt that it was an unglamorous business, but it was all totally new to me."

One thing Brenda did quickly find out and greatly appreciated was that the Turnbows were a bonded, loving family, and that family togetherness was their first priority. "Lee and Evelyne and Randy and Steve were a very loving family. To an outsider like me that was very appealing. It was certainly something I wanted to be a part of." So in 1965, Randy and Brenda were married at Bixby Knolls Christian Church and began applying the next layer of strength and stability to the family.

While EME was still a faraway dream, it was clear from the beginning of their marriage that planning for its future was a huge priority to Randy. "When we got married, I knew a little more about the business and I wanted to be supportive, of course. Randy explained that we couldn't buy a house right at the beginning because he was saving up for his own business. He said we needed a five-year plan, sort of like the Soviets were doing at the time, to plan everything out in our household," Brenda said. "After the first five years, it seemed like many of our friends had bought a house, but Randy said we weren't quite there yet and we needed a second five-year plan. I agreed, but put my foot down; there would be no third five-year plan."

Randy was well into his aerospace finishing career by the early 1970s, working with his dad at California Metal Processing, as well as working second and third jobs at Alert Metal Finishing and AAA metal finishing as a salesman. He was intent on improving the skills he had learned as a teenager so that he could move on to his next career, his ultimate goal, owning and running his own metal finishing company. But how and where and when this was to occur was only known by God. All Randy could do was follow the signs.

"I had tried to buy AAA metal finishing and a couple of other local companies, but nothing ever worked out," Randy said. "I had known Brenda since junior high and she had plenty of family here, with her sister only a few blocks away. I liked Southern California and nobody was offering me a chance to move, so I figured I was going to stay. The question was, stay and do what?"

Brenda and Randy had already started their own family, first with a baby girl, Rhanda, followed by three boys, Wesley, Dalton and later, John Travis. The unshakeable family bonds were growing deeper and wider in the Turnbow family. Steve, younger than Randy by three years, had married his sweetheart Melody and had had a son, whom they named Bryan. Learning from his father's edict, and his older brother's example, Steve had graduated from the Northrop's Technical University and was working as a helicopter mechanic at the Long Beach Airport.

The family was now firmly planted in the Long Beach area. The layers were growing and strengthening, and the only question remaining was, what was the next big family step? The answer came in a phone call Randy took from a local businessman, Bob Butler, late in 1971. Would Randy have any interest in buying a local metal finishing company of his, located in the nearby town of Compton, California, a company named E.M.E., Inc.?

EME was still a fairly new company, having been founded in 1962. But the price was right. The timing was optimal. It specialized in the career Randy loved and had proven he could succeed in. Plus, it offered him the opportunity to fulfill what he said he had always wanted to do in his chosen profession; own and be the boss of his own metal finishing shop, something that had first been relayed to him by his granddad, Walter Hamilton, and then delivered to him daily by his dad, Lee.

Would Randy have any interest in purchasing EME in Compton? Yes, indeed, he very well might. The next chapter in the Turnbow family story was about to begin.

CHAPTER 2

EME's Humble Beginnings: Dreams and Debt

"In February of 1972, I paid Bob Butler $4,000 for EME. It was too much!" Randy joked. The price had seemed fair enough at the time, and its purchase did fulfill his dream of owning and operating his own company, but there were surprises and unseen frustrations ahead. Unbeknownst to him Bob owed a year's worth of rent to the landlord, thousands of dollars to financial creditors, and there were even a few absentee co-owners that were never mentioned. "Even the company name was quirky," Randy recalled. "When I asked Bob what EME stood for he said that it was short for Electro-Machine and Engineering. I joked back and said, 'Since we don't do electrics, machining or engineering, I see why you just stick to EME.'"

Randy had also inherited three employees with the company, which was two too many for the quickly sinking company. But typical of the Turnbow spirit, hardened and determined to achieve his dream, Randy quickly did what had to be done. "By the end of the first week I had let go of the two production employees and had only kept the secretary, simply because I needed somebody to answer the phone," Randy said.

His next move turned out to be one of his most important, one that is still paying dividends today. He called on an old friend, Rudy Munguia. Randy had known Rudy from his early days in the metal finishing business and persuaded him to accept his offer as the first official EME employee. "Rudy knew how to run every kind of plating there was for any type of industry or job," Randy said. "He was an invaluable help, especially in the early years, and stayed with me for the rest of his career. Today, his brother Danny still works for me as a master painter."

Danny Munguia said that his brother, who has been slowed by health challenges in recent years, always speaks with pride of those early, sometimes dark, days of EME. "Every time I talk to my brother, he asks how Randy is doing, how Steve is doing. He always wants to know everything about the company. He wants to know how it is going. He is very happy and very proud of all the success we have had." Danny says he learned early on the secrets of the company's success, both then and now: love and hard work. "I love these people and they love me. I always try to do my best to see the company succeeds."

With his one key employee in place to help perform the plating, and somebody to answer the phone, it was up to Randy to do the rest. "That left me to rebuild the shop, literally: find customers, pick up the parts, do all the processing work, deliver them back, print the billing and seek new approvals for new processes," he explained. "I worked 12-16 hours a day, seven days a week, but it wasn't all that bad. I had a beautiful, loving and supportive wife and two wonderful kids at the time. And at age 26, I was free. I made all the business decisions and succeeded or failed by my own hand, which was what I had always wanted to do."

Luckily, in these early days of EME, the industry was not nearly as complicated or as technical as it is now. "There was a time when the words used in the aerospace industry made sense to the common man. Words like, 'form, fit and function' drove the industry." Steve said. There were no reams of instructions or government documents to fill out or follow. The person who knew the right guy and worked the fastest and the hardest got the job. These were Turnbow family strengths.

Randy was able to use his industry sources and rely on the relationships he had formed while working for a decade in the metal finishing trade. The people he had met through his dad and on his own now became a key part of the early Turnbow success. "Randy knew lots of aerospace people and was able to get the first aerospace prime contractor approvals fast, just because of his contacts," Steve said.

"In those days, items had to be delivered in a cost effective manner to meet End Item Testing Requirements." Working with less than optimum equipment in small, cramped facilities, without computers, technical manuals and high tech chemicals was a challenge to say the least. Yet surprisingly, EME was able to accomplish things never before attempted in the business quickly and for little money, which pleased their clients and resulted in immediate approvals.

Perhaps the biggest surprise, and the biggest blessing in the initial growth of EME, came barely six months after Randy had taken over the company. He was working in the small facility one day when he saw his father, Lee, stroll up the front driveway of the small company. "Hey Pops, what are you doing here?" Randy asked his mentor. His dad's reply stunned him. "I'm working for you now." With his business still in survival mode, Randy became flustered. He told his dad that there was no money to pay him with and that he should not have quit his job without discussing it together. "Don't tell me your troubles. I've already got work on the way over here," Lee replied.

"If you knew Lee you would understand that this impulsive move was not unusual. He was quite a character and very compulsive and independent," Randy said. Lee had been a salesman for an EME competitor, but when he saw the chance to work with his son at his company, he couldn't pass up the chance. "Financial security was always number one priority to him, but despite the risk, Lee began to work at EME just six months after Randy purchased it and stayed there the rest of his life," Evelyne said. "What more could I ask for, to see my family work together? So many families have problems or don't like each other. It's a blessing."

Lee had worked in the plating industry most of his life, since arriving in California at age 16, and was well known in the local industry of aerospace metal finishing. Early on, Lee's talents with machines and his connections to people and key customers proved to be very beneficial to the company. Lee quickly became an invaluable asset to the company.

"My dad was physically gifted. He could work on anything, build anything, do anything," Randy said. Due to his Depression-era roots, Lee knew how to find, bargain and salvage anything that others had thrown away. On a very limited budget, or no budget at all, Lee worked hard to find needed building supplies, while Randy acted as the company's one-man sales and processing and delivery team. "This started a long and fruitful relationship between me and my dad, and we worked together all the rest of his life. He was a genius in so many ways, especially in the construction and maintenance of just about everything," Randy said.

Knowing his son's limited financial condition, Lee never asked Randy for a nickel as an employee. Instead, Lee leased to EME some of the equipment that it needed. This agreement set Lee and Evelyne up financially even in their later years, and also helped EME immediately. Equipment was definitely one of EME's weaknesses at the time.

Often Randy would go out in his old pick-up truck, which had been hit from several different angles, to pick up jobs, parts or supplies. He would travel the Southern California roads in that truck while looking for new work and taking care of old and new customers. The 'original' headquarters, which Randy would return to from these deliveries, was also decidedly humble. The rented building was a mere 3,750 square feet. They would have to conduct business both inside and out because there was not enough covered space for even the small number of employees they had.

The first chance at expansion came in 1974, two years after the original purchase. EME's landlord, Mr. Neeley, now fully paid, offered Randy a chance to buy the small property they were renting and also purchase three other pieces of property in the area. They chose to take that deal, and immediately began to enlarge the footprint of EME.

Hard work and dedicated employees like Rudy Mungia, factored into early success for the new company, or at least enough success to get it off the critical list. Rudy, the original new employee, was so dedicated to EME's welfare that he moved into a small house located on the EME property where he acted as an unofficial security guard for the company. It was common for thieves to break into companies and steal parts to sell for scrap metal. Rudy knew that if anything bad happened to EME, it affected him as well. So Rudy took an active part in securing EME property at night.

Having an employee's home on company property had other perks as well. Often on Friday night, Rudy would have everyone over to his house to celebrate the week's work and to encourage the small band of new employees. It was their commitment and willingness to take chances that was furthering EME's success. "As time went by, EME continued to grow and prosper," Randy recalled. "Well, prosper might be a bit strong", he said smiling, "but we did pay the bills and had enough left over to expand some and take care of our families."

The property at 431 E. Oaks St. in Compton California was slowly growing. Eventually Randy and the company purchased the property directly north of the current facility and that enabled EME to expand to the next street over. "With the new property we were able to build a new state-of-the-art paint building. My guys built this outer building right here," Randy said, pointing to a huge metal structure while making his daily morning walking tour of the facilities. "We ordered the steel building from Arkansas, and it came in a huge flat-bed truck one day. That truck just pulled up to the side of the property and dumped everything right here. Wow, we didn't know what we were going to do with all the parts and pieces, but eventually we built that 10,000 sq. ft. building with our own hands. Lee and Steve and our entire crew all working together on the project put it together in record time." In addition, Randy hired a well know architect named Peter Porter to design a new contemporary office complex. He did a great job incorporating the feel of the aerospace industry into the outer design. With the addition of the new paint shop and modern headquarters building, EME now has buildings inclosing 90,000 square feet, and total property extending clear through the city block with addresses on both streets.

The new company became increasingly known for processing complicated parts that no one else was willing to tackle, especially large or heavy parts. As a result, they were awarded one of the largest parts ever to be "electro-polished" in history, stainless steel missile body parts. These tubes were two feet in diameter and 30 feet long. Using a cleaver contraption, which slowly rotated the part while it was suspended in a horse trough lined with plastic and filled with plating solution, the 30-foot parts were chemically polished both inside and out at the same time. EME had found their niche in the field of metal finishing and plating.

After the first five years of owning E.M.E., Inc., Randy was finally beginning to see a glimmer of the hope of success. In order for his small company to really take off, however, a third key player needed to be brought on board.

CHAPTER 3

Steve Joins the Turnbow Team

The addition of Steve Turnbow, the third key member of the EME family, did not come through an offer to buy a company or by simply walking up the driveway, but by telephone.

Randy heard that Steve, who had previously been employed at the Long Beach airport, and now employed by one of EME's customers, had been laid off. With his fledgling company just five years old and beginning to enjoy its first taste of success, Randy decided to ask his brother if he would work with him temporarily until he found another job. Separated in age by only three years, the two brothers grew up together in Lakewood and had remained close through the years. And with their father's credo of family-togetherness ever on his mind, Randy was eager to give Steve a chance.

"Dad was big on family loyalty. Steve and I felt we had to take care of each other. I have tried to pass that on to my own kids as well." This turned out to be one of EME's best decisions ever, and a key turning point in the history of the company. The Turnbow men—Lee, Randy and Steve—were now not only family, but comrades, working at the same company, and seeking success together.

"Over the years many different people would have a profound effect on the building and growing of EME. But as I look back on those early years, I consider it to be God's true blessing to allow the three of us to work together and build the company we enjoy today."

One important key to the family company's success was the fact that Lee, Steve and Randy were expertly skilled— all in different areas. Lee was the ultimate fix-it man, willing and able to use his years of experience and ingenuity to build, create or repair any piece of machinery the company needed. Steve was brilliant in the area of chemicals, processing and quality control. He could derive any formula, any equation, or any adaptation needed to complete a job most people would consider impossible.

"I'm definitely more the mad scientist type, with all the technical data. For some reason, I retain trade knowledge for decades. If we have more production or inventory needs, I am able to retain the knowledge and use it," Steve said. Randy was the full-time salesman, working with customers, seeking new people to serve, picking up and delivering jobs and overseeing the small, but steadily growing company. "Randy really is the face or the front end of the company. I have the back end in the laboratory," Steve said. "It's a very interesting situation working with the family, but it's really a great blessing."

From starting the company with just three people who had to race around putting out one fire after another just to keep EME afloat, the teaming up of the Turnbow men allowed each one of them to concentrate on what they did the best. "Steve is much better running things day to day," Randy said. "I tend focus on the new ideas and big picture. Steve is a genius with chemicals and understanding chemical and paint processes. My dad was a master of things mechanical and was physically gifted enough to design and make almost anything."

"I think we all take responsibility to make sure it's a team effort," said Steve. "Randy was the big boss, hiring and firing and doing what he felt was necessary. I was always reading all the specifications and prime contractor documents. I would also process parts with the guys. "It was a joy for me to actually run the parts myself. I was the chemical processing question-

and-answer go-to guy, and the little boss. With a small crew, very little money, and Randy as our fearless leader, we pressed on to an uncertain future."

Along with his chemical genius, Steve brought to EME a heart that cared deeply for its employees. "Steve was always more caring of our employees' safety and well-being than I was. This has led all of us at EME to consider the needs of our folks' welfare." "We consider ourselves a place that treats our employees better," Randy added. "When you think of a good place to come to work, you think of EME."

Good treatment of employees was a reflection of how the Turnbow men treated each other. They were not only family, but friends. "I asked Dalton one time what it was like to work with all of this family and he said, 'You can hear Dad and Uncle Steve laughing all over the shop.'" Evelyne says. "We are always working together," Steve added, "on a human relationship level, that's the way it's always been. The secret of our relationship lasting so long is that we have remained respectful of each other all of these years."

In the late 1970s, with the Turnbow trio working together, the new EME metal finishing company became an unstoppable Southern California business force. "Dad always said about Steve and him and I, that any two of us could be successful, but all three of

us could take over the world," said Randy. As the Turnbow men used their talents to divide and conquer the metal finishing industry, the focus of the company became clearer during those years. EME steadily gained the reputation for taking on jobs nobody else would attempt. In 1978 they were asked to silver-plate a nuclear submarine shaft bearing which measured eight feet in diameter and weighed 1,200 pounds. At the time it was known as the largest part ever to be silver coated. A huge project like this, with large military and government implications, could literally make or break a small company like EME. But if successful, it would make them the envy of their well-established competitors. This was an opportunity for the Turnbows to shine and they accepted the challenge that no one else would dare attempt, even though they were not quite sure how it would be accomplished.

Because of the unique size of the project, no one in America seemed to have the right size tanks for this procedure. So the high school educated Lee, with a PhD in real world work and business skills, devised and built a special tank just for that one coating process. Steve, as usual, put on his mad scientist hat, came up with the exact formula for the process, had the right chemical balance, and controlled the whole process from the tank so that he could maintain that precise balance. Randy was in charge of purchasing everything that was needed to process a plating part of that dimension. After extensive research he determined that a secret road trip was in order. He traveled to San Francisco to buy one of the largest anodizing rectifiers, previously used of course, and originally owned by the Navy.

For another difficult job, the Turnbow trio worked alone on Sundays, so their neighbors and fellow competitors would not find out what they were up to. Steve and Randy had cleverly devised a method to electroless nickel-plate a certain part. They did it by pumping the chemical solution that Steve had devised through a plastic children's swimming pool. Then Steve and

Randy sat in their swim trunks in a couple of old lawn chairs to keep watch over the process, making sure it was working as planned.

On yet another occasion, they used a new special tank designed by Lee to anodize aluminum rings used for building the disposable fuel tanks on the space shuttle. These rings weighed 4,000 pound each, and no one else in the country would tackle them. But on one of their infamous undercover weekends at the shop, EME once again accomplished what no other metal finishing company would even attempt!

The success reverberated across the entire industry and the days of bleak survival soon became a thing of the past. Now it was mission accomplished, projects completed, and bring on the next impossible assignment for EME to tackle! EME was now a serious contender, but success brought on new dilemmas. They were now in need of a primer and paint shop.

The answer to that problem came from another family member. Brenda's sister, Sandy, was married to Ken Jeglum. At the time Ken was working for a large spray paint gun manufacturing company. "Hearing me say that I was going to need a primer and paint shop addition, Ken asked me if he could paint for EME as a subcontractor," Randy recalled. The plan seemed good to everyone, and for convenience Ken moved into an empty building inside EME. This arrangement worked well for many years, until the two companies decided to go their separate ways. EME built three of its own paint buildings over time and Ken established another successful aerospace company called Alloy Processing.

A few years later EME was called on again to make the impossible possible, as Boeing, one of the company's prime suppliers of work, invented a whole new kind of boric-sulfuric acid anodize for aluminum aircraft components. Thanks to the company's and the Turnbows' reputation, EME was granted a franchise to perform the process for Boeing and was, for many years, the only private company doing this special anodizing process. "We had the resources, the people and the equipment to do the job," Steve said. "We were a just-in-time business and, working together, we were able to get everything done."

The tank line that Lee helped design and build for the boric-sulfuric anodize process is still being used for that purpose. As some of the largest tanks around, they make it possible for EME to work on the new Boeing 787 Dreamliner, which is the first commercial plane in history to "exclusively" use the new nearly pollution-free anodize coating. Again, it was the EME-Turnbow trio leading the way. Their specified talents appeared miraculously designed to be compatible, and it seemed they could only lead to success.

As the company entered its second decade in the 1980s, there arose the growing need for job training, in order to comply with the government and some of the largest contractors. "What we do is pretty specialized stuff. Steve now handles all of the training, which is also pretty specialized, because it has to be documented and formatted for the government and other customers," said Randy. Steve set up a special training room at the ever-growing EME facilities, in order to teach the technical knowledge he was already familiar with, and to interact with the new employees, and to keep in touch with the veterans of the company.

"I feel training is what allowed EME to rise to the heights," said Steve. "I feel like I've spent 80 percent of my life training. New employees come into entry level jobs and move up to become our top leadership. We have staff management, training meetings, and reach out to all the employees, like they are our brothers and sisters. We work together to do what we can't do alone, and we're free to have fun while we're doing this." This extensive training, led by Steve and overseen by Randy and others, has enabled EME to get many big government contracts, which are usually larger in quantity and offer a steadier flow of work.

At this time of heavy employee training, Steve and Randy were also beginning to train the next generation of Turnbow leadership, just as their father had trained them. During the summers, each one of Randy's children, Wesley, Dalton and John, along with his daughter Rhanda, would work briefly there, doing various odd jobs and getting a taste of the family company. "I did maintenance and bookkeeping at EME on several different summers during high school and college," Wesley Turnbow added.

Steve's son Bryan also worked there a week or two in the summers, learning about what the older Turnbow generation was doing on a daily basis, and about what they hoped to accomplish in the future. "Seeing the company through my dad's eyes is really interesting," Bryan Turnbow said. "I'm very proud of what the family has produced and the way EME has defied the odds for 50 years and made a difference."

Some of the younger generation chose to play a role in the future of EME. Some chose to pursue different careers, but all were exposed to the Turnbow family way. "There were a lot of opportunities to work at EME full-time, but no pressure to do it," Bryan said. "The family backbone has carried us. It has left the business steady. The family here is the story forever."

Randy's dad showing up unexpectedly on EME's front driveway to work for him had become a significant pillar in the success of the family business. Convincing Steve to take a "temporary" assignment while looking for something better, became an equally, if not more significant pillar. Randy recently asked Steve if he was still look for something better or if he was planning to finally commit to staying after 35 years. "I sure hope he stays," Randy joked.

The story of EME's success was not dependent on Turnbow family members alone however. There was a third pillar—the ever-growing family of longtime and dedicated employees who simply showed up one day for a menial job and ended up staying for a meaningful career.

CHAPTER 4

Long-Term Employees Lead to Long-Term Success

Behind the long-term success of EME, Inc., there are more than a handful of blood relatives with the same last name. Throughout the course of EME's successful history, there have been many employees who have contributed immensely to the progress of the company. They have come and stayed, becoming not merely temporary employees but friends, and part of the family.

"It's a really, really good team," said Dalton. "I think that's how God has helped us in so many different situations." From consisting of one trusted friend and one person to answer the phone, to employing more than 130 dedicated men and women, all working together, the Turnbows have faithfully grown their family to also include these friends and co-workers. "I could never mention all the folks who have helped make EME what it is today," Randy said. "When employees are your friends it makes a huge difference."

Employees love working at EME, even though it is sometimes necessary to let them go. "I can't get people to leave here. I fire them and they keep coming back a few months later to see if I've changed my mind. It's really incredible," he said.

Juan Chavez is currently the longest tenured EME employee, at 31 years, followed closely by **Danny Munguia**, the brother of Randy's original hire, with 30 years. **Elias Avila** and **Guillermo Diaz** are close behind, with 29 years of service. Within the 30 longest-working employees alone there is a total of 575 years of service! The original hire of **Rudy Munguia** and later of his brother Danny highlights another key principal of the company's over the years. Not only is hiring at EME mainly word of mouth, but it's mainly word of mouth through current families.

"We have a lot of family here," Quality Control Manager **John Lopez, Sr.,** said. "Everybody works for somebody and everybody is related. It's been a great success for us, a great source of pride." Lopez's son, **John Lopez, Jr.,** came to work at EME seven years ago. He did such an excellent job, that he received a series of rapid promotions and has now become his father's boss as Quality Assurance Manager. "They offered me the job, but I knew he (John, Jr.,) would do it better than me," John, Sr., said.

John, Sr.'s path to EME is typical of many who came to the company briefly and then wound up staying for a lifetime. "I first heard about EME from a temporary agency. They were looking for someone to paint houses in Compton. Nobody looking for a job at the agency raised their hand because Compton didn't have the best reputation back then. When the boss got to me, he asked if I wanted to go to Compton, and I told him I was here to work so I was glad to go."

John, Sr.'s first impression was puzzling to say the least. He was told there was much painting going on, but there were no houses anywhere. "I thought I was in the wrong place, but they welcomed me in," he said. "What I ended up finding out was if you can't work here, you can't work anywhere. The first day I vacuumed waste water off the floor. Then I did something else and then something different after that. They eventually asked if I wanted a full-time job, and I said, 'That's why I'm here'. I showed up to paint a house and ended up staying for 30 years."

This was not by accident. The Turnbow family saw something good in John Lopez Sr. and chose to mentor him, as well as many others they thought had potential, in order to create a strong EME family — one that would last through thick and thin. "Steve soon asked me if I wanted to try something else, and I told him I didn't know how, but he promised to teach me. Steve has been the greatest mentor in my life. He has a bigger heart for employees than anybody I've ever seen. He's meant everything to me," John Sr., said.

After starting with maintenance and vacuuming chemicals, John, Sr. then moved on to penetrant inspection and later, dyeing backpacks was processing for the Army. As a result of their success with other large military projects, EME had been asked to anodize and dye more than 1 million metal backpacks olive green for the U.S. Army, to be used for overseas combat duty. This contract was so large that EME had to hire many more people and begin working 24-7 for several years to complete it. John was one of the key players in this endeavor, and as a result, is able to enjoy the fact that his work will go down in history. "I even heard there was one in the Smithsonian Museum in Washington, D.C.," Lopez said. These were good times, and at EME, there were many of those.

But like the larger, extended family they are, EME stood by Lopez during tough times as well. His first wife, Gloria who also worked at EME, was one day shot and tragically killed. John, Sr. also battled addiction problems as well, but EME cared for him all along the way. "Now, Randy has passed along that personal caring to his sons also. They have really taken care of their employees," he said. "If that's not right, then nothing is right. It makes it easy to come to work in the morning when you have people like that."

The Marketplace Chaplains program, which Randy brought into the company several years ago, has been another example of the caring environment fostered at EME. John, Sr. said, "I was initially against the chaplain program because I thought it would get in the way. But Randy came to me and said, 'just let me know how it's going.' The chaplains have worked out great because it shows that the company cares for people. I was wrong about them."

John's story is one of many in a company with numerous faithful workers. **Elias Avila**, another long-term employee, began work in April 1982 when EME had less than three dozen employees and one magnetic and penetrant line. He stayed for the same reason so many others have—the positive working environment. At EME, if you worked hard, you were rewarded, and promoted when possible.

"When I first came here, the people welcomed me, and I started right away. I worked in plating and made sure I always did my job. I moved over to fork lift operator and always made sure I did my job. I was always willing to work, and I think we have bosses who work well with people. I want to help people that help us."

Operations Manager, **Jesus Silva**, said he's only had one job in his whole life—working at EME. He has been here for 23 years, and he isn't looking to leave any time soon. "This is the only job I've had. This is home to me." He heard about the job opening at EME like so many others, through a satisfied family member. "My older, Jose, told me about the job and said they needed somebody, and I'm glad they did," Jesus said. "We are a company who embraces family and wants more family when we have an opening. That's where we go look for people."

Jesus has another brother, Frank Anguiano, who works and supervises maintenance at the company. Here, like in the rest of the departments, they are encouraged to care about more than just making a paycheck or just doing a job. "I have so much respect for Steve and Randy", Jesus stated. "They taught me about life as well as about metal finishing."

With a large number of Hispanics in the EME workforce, Jesus said that the company has been quick to embrace a progressive business model. "We are in a very competitive industry, and now Latinos are starting to move up the ladder in plating companies around the country. Steve was one of the first to recognize this and was eager to promote us. We are able to relate well to our Latino customers because of our similar backgrounds."

"Steve is the one who taught me how to treat people with respect and professionalism. And if you can make money and help people along the way, that's the best of both worlds. When I started here, I was making $4.50 an hour as a sandblaster, and I was probably overpaid at that, but they always stood by me." He added, "We are here today because of Steve and Randy and the initial vision they had for this company and we must never forget that."

Steve said that it is these long-term employees who have helped ensure the company's long-term success. "Without good employees here, we are just a bunch of tanks, chemicals and walls," he said. "We have worked hard to keep the family feeling and to protect each other's back and the gains we have made," Jesus added.

Former Air Force Lieutenant Colonel and current EME employee, **Jim Baker**, met the Turnbow family in the fourth grade, when he started playing Little League baseball with Steve in Lakewood, California. "I went into the Air Force after college, but always kept in contact with Steve over Christmas," Jim said. "I knew the company was growing and he was enjoying working with his brother."

Baker spent four years in the Air Force before leaving in 1976, when he briefly worked for commercial airlines. After being laid off in Texas, he went back to the Air Force where he flew B-52 and B-1 Bombers. He also spent time at the Pentagon in Washington, D.C., from 1992 to 1995, where he worked with the Emergency Action Message, a system that could send the U.S. to war at a moment's notice. "That was a lot of pressure. I was glad to leave," he said.

During the Christmas of 1996, as Jim prepared to retire from the Air Force, he talked with Steve who asked him a question:

would he come to work for EME and help modernize the company with his extensive computer knowledge? This turned out to be another wise decision. Jim immediately fit in well with the management team, and was able to update the growing company with his computer training, while formalizing protocol using his military background.

When Baker arrived at EME headquarters, he found the working conditions much different than he had had in the Air Force. "When I started out [at EME], we didn't have a lot of forms. There was a lot more structure in the Air Force. We had people who knew what to do and how to do it here, but it wasn't written down." Because so many employees had been there for so long, there were very few written documents or procedures, just a general knowledge of the way things had always been done, passed on from one employee to another, which is often referred to as tribal knowledge.

This method had worked well in the early days of the growing company, but as the industry was modernizing, expanding, and becoming more and more regulated by the government, the lack of formal documentation was becoming an issue. The computer system at EME was very basic as well, and Baker worked hard to help modernize and streamline the company. "Before all the structure was in place, we were always weighing quality vs. production, but now it's just down to maintenance," Jim said. Once again, the right person had come along at the right time in order to ensure the continued success of EME. This was becoming a pattern in the company's history.

When **Manuel Gaxiola**, the current supervisor of shipping and receiving, arrived at EME 28 years ago, he didn't have far to travel. EME was located literally a street away from his boyhood home. "I have a good friend who used to be a manager here and he helped get me hired in 1985. That was my first job in the industry, and it's been a good one because we have good parts, quality people and we take care of the customers. That's a good combination."

Gaxiola is responsible for getting the EME trucks on the road every day to deliver customer product and for working with customer requests. He also works as a final inspector. "Every year seems to get better because the company is growing from leadership at the top," he said. He liked his job so much that he got his sister, Maria, a job in the masking department.

Manuel has always found the presence of family, starting with Steve and Randy, and filtering down to include the rest of the family and long-term employees, to be a positive thing. "We have good communication with the Turnbows, a good understanding. I like the environment, and the people are good to work with. Lee could build anything, he was quite a character who could become your friend," Gaxiola said. "Dalton and Wesley are great guys to work for, because they are willing to listen and help you." As he nears his fourth decade of EME service, he states that the future looks brighter than ever. "The aerospace industry looks forward and we are always looking to the next level. I think the future looks very good at this time."

Frank Anguiano is the third brother from his family to have worked at EME. He began in the summer of 1990 and has never regretted the 22 years he has spent at the company. "I do the plumbing and the maintenance and just try to keep the company going. I don't ever get bored because there is always something going on here. At first, I just helped clean up around here. Then I drove a fork lift, worked with blueprints, and anything else they asked me to do. It feels good to be around here because Randy and everybody have been good to me, even when you have problems."

Like anyone who has been at the company for decades, Auguiano was willing to do whatever it took to help EME move forward. He helped design and build an overhead crane, helped build production lines, and built a special new sandblaster in 1999. "I always like a new challenge. We've even moved different rooms around to build a super paint line scrubber. I try to just do it better for the company. Just try to keep it going."

Randy had known **Eloy Sandoval** since the 1970s, not as a friend or a co-worker, but as the president of his largest competitor. "I had never thought much about Eloy becoming an employee. The idea of hiring Eloy never crossed my mind. Why would it? He was my competitor. But the good Lord had a different plan, and when Eloy sold his company and asked me about a job, of course I hired him."

When he arrived in 1995 to become EME's new sales manager, Eloy was equipped to benefit the company in many ways. Having previously owned a plating company, he knew the business thoroughly and had inside knowledge of industry customers. He also had the necessary contacts that would allow EME to continue to grow. "We have good people, a good company and good employees. When I was president of my own company, I was exposed to all kinds of rules and all kinds of jobs. I've been privileged to see the growth of this company up close from inside and also from afar."

"As sales manager, Eloy is responsible for the 20 largest accounts, but is always on the look-out for new business," Randy said. "He is smart and loyal and knew more about this business than anyone else I had ever met. Over the many years we have worked together, he has proved to be a wonderful salesman and a good friend as well."

While there have been too many dedicated employees to mention all by name, Randy said it would be a mistake to not mention the many female personnel which have helped make EME a success. EME has always had a large percentage of women working on many different jobs.

Barbara Greybehl was perhaps the most key. She spent some 18 years working as the financial controller at EME. Barbara was fiercely loyal to Randy and she was of absolute trustworthiness until her day of retirement.

"A current employee named **Ellie Chairez** has managed the critical masking department better than anyone ever has and I am thankful for her," Randy stated. "Great inspectors of finished products include **Claudia Martinez** and **Christina Garcia**. Three other women I want to mention are **Espie Ramirez**, who prices all the jobs internally and quotes most of the parts for our customers, and **Maria Favela**, who works along with her. Also, **Margaret Hammonds**, who follows in Barbara's footsteps as dedicated and trustworthy in the position of bookkeeping and payroll. These women are truly invaluable to our company, as are the ladies who create the technically complex shop travelers and customer job certifications, as well as those whom mask, unmask, inspect and package our finished parts."

The contributions of many too numerous to count have helped build this company from humble beginnings to its current successful state. "Over the years, EME has employed hundreds of people, and I wish I could mention so many more that have brought their talents and skills here," Randy said. With the company led by men full of faith, love and honor, and with all of these committed, hard-working employees in place, EME was equipped to weather any storm that life could bring upon them. And it was because of this unified team, and by the grace of God, that the company withstood the most trying times of its history.

"Without their dedication and hard work, we would not have survived."

CHAPTER 5

Difficult Times Transform EME

As previously explained, the purpose of metal finishing is to add one or more layers of finishing in order to protect and strengthen the material. This prepares it to withstand the most intense stress. The finishing makes sure that the more extreme the situation it is put in, and the more volatile the environment, the better the material will hold up and not crack or fail under the pressure.

Just as the Turnbows and EME have used this layering method to protect the parts they have treated over the life of the 50 year-old company, so have they built up the company itself—with layers of faith, love for family, and love for others—in order to withstand the extreme pressures and trials of the industry. This was wise on the part of the Turnbow family, because running a growing a company turned out to be extremely difficult. The process of resurrecting a company that was near bankruptcy in the early 1970s was only the birth pangs.

After the company was "reborn", there were many more trials and troubles the Turnbows would face as it grew from infancy and childhood into a mature, stable company—including aerospace downturns, union votes and employee strikes, street riots, and rigorous inspections. "We have had every kind of problem you could imagine, but the Good Lord has always seen us through," Randy said.

After two of the three original employees had been laid off and a trusted friend, Rudy Munguia, was hired, the first hurdle for the small, cramped company faced was its location. As John Lopez, Sr. mentioned before, when he first came here in the early 1970s, the City of Compton had a reputation for high crime and violence, and it wasn't getting any better. "Even people who knew the community, like Randy, took their lives in their own hands in order to build a business from almost nothing with their own wit, skills, education and determination," Steve added.

The city government was having problems, which meant the city police force was as well. Changes did not really come until the Compton City Police were disbanded in the year 2000, and their duties were transferred to the Los Angeles County Sheriff's Department. In the city crime reduced although any incidents could occur.

"We had a few incidents of vandalism and graffiti." Once, Randy even came to work to find bullet holes in his office upstairs with one actually lodged in the picture frame in his office. "But now that the Sheriff's Department took over the patrols, we haven't had any problems," Randy said.

In order to prevent any internal problems, Randy knew he had to take swift, forceful action whenever an issue came to light. "One day we had graffiti in the bathroom and I couldn't find out who did it. So I brought everybody together and told them I was sending them home for the day until somebody fixed the damage. I told them exactly what kind of paint I wanted in the bathroom, what color and what I wanted it to look like when it was finished." Faced with a most unwanted vacation on payday, the bathroom was quickly repaired by employees to exact specifications. That was the last time there was any kind of internal graffiti trouble at EME." Randy said.

Several years later, the Turnbows and EME faced a more serious kind of challenge when a majority of the company's workforce went on a "wildcat" strike. According to a California state law, employees were now able to vote a union into a company. A company could not be forced to have a union, but the employees could immediately go on strike. A strike could paralyze the company because the replacements they would need to hire would have to be willing to cross the picket line. In Compton those picket lines were very dangerous.

"We had 85 percent of the company go out on strike because some of the guys convinced people they had to have a union and were not being treated fairly at EME," Randy recalled. After more than a decade of working on improving the company and the lives of its employees, Randy was equally convinced that a union was not necessary and would ruin the family atmosphere he had worked so hard to build. Over a few days a stalemate ensued, with neither side willing to budge from their position.

Finally, in an attempt to break the impasse, Randy visited one of the strike leader's homes, and standing on his porch delivered a powerful message to many of the employees gathered there. "I told them I didn't care if I lost the entire company. We weren't going to have a union here. They knew I wasn't bluffing because I had already done some other things (like the graffiti in the bathroom), so they knew I was serious." Within a few days the union was voted down and the strike was over, the majority of the employees came to work and EME continued moving toward success.

Following the strike, however, approximately 40 employees, including many of the strike organizers, left the company and filed false workman's compensation claims against EME, mostly in different counties to make it hard to track. Because of the large number of claims against his company, Randy's worker's compensation insurance claims for the following years went up 400%, a figure which could have bankrupted the company. "It's just something we could not take and be able to survive," Randy said.

His solution was one which would have made his dad Lee— who specialized in making the impossible possible on limited resources—very proud. Randy started his own temporary work agency called Talent Today, chartered under his brother's name.

"While it's something you could not easily do today, we did it back then for several years. That saved us because we were able to hire employees from the temporary agency and have no employee or worker's compensation claims against EME." Another problem solved by Turnbow ingenuity and street-smarts.

Even though the walk-out had been very painful and financially troubling due to some of the employees, it must be said that over the years, the majority of their employees have been very supportive and helpful to the company. For example, during the 1992 Los Angeles riots—sparked by the Rodney King beating and the acquittal of the involved police officers—rioting, looting and destruction broke out all over the Los Angeles area, including Long Beach and Compton.

"When our payroll service said they would not bring the employee paychecks into the riot-zone," Randy said, "I got in my car, grabbed my shotgun, picked up the checks myself, and drove them into Compton to give to my folks. I knew they needed their wages for their families to live on." The next day, over 20 employees volunteered to protect EME around the clock, with shotguns and other firearms, until it was safe to come back to work. "Nobody is going to burn our company down as long as we have any way to stop them," said one of Randy's long-time workers. The riots subsided, and EME was once again able to resume production.

But the greatest man-made crisis ever to hit the company was still to come. It tested every fiber and strength of every family member there, but it also turned into a transformational event for EME, which still reverberates in the company walls today.

As the aerospace industry continued to grow more complex and more specialized, some of the largest defense and aerospace contractors, known in the industry as the primes, got together to form an international accreditation agency called Nadcap—the National Aerospace and Defense Contractors Accreditation Program. Nadcap was created in 1990 and is now the leading, worldwide cooperative inspection program of major aerospace companies. It was designed to manage a cost-effective consensus approach to regulating special processes and production, and for furthering improvement within the industry.

In laymen's terms, in order to work on government, any large industry, or prime project, Nadcap certification had to be gained and maintained. To not have this certification meant losing your work and most likely, your company. EME had learned its trade by hard work, on-site learning, and hands-on experience. Little was written down. Information was primarily passed on by word of mouth and through job training. They had decades-worth of proof of their good work by their many satisfied customers, but the conglomerate of large companies now wanted many details.

EME was able to obtain certification early in Nadcap history, retain it for several years, but each year it became more difficult to pass the inspections. Nadcap continually increased their quality and documentation requirements, and more was expected of a compliant company the longer it was certified.

Then, in 2007, the bomb dropped. Inspection time came during the summer, and Nadcap assigned EME a person who had failed numerous companies in the past and would go on to fail many more. "They sent the killer inspector of all time and he wrote us up for everything we could imagine," Baker said. The news was swift and devastating. EME had lost its certification, work was not to be sent there, and it could soon be out of business.

"Losing Nadcap was very hard. We had to lay off a lot of people. I'm usually not an emotional guy, but I got very emotional laying off a lot of good people," Jesus Silva said. The once-booming work force of more than 125 people was suddenly cut by more than half with very little work to do. "When we lost Nadcap certification in 2007, that was one of the toughest situations we had ever been through as a company," Dalton Turnbow said.

"We had to lay off 75 people in two weeks and I was here for every one of them. It was very difficult and heart-wrenching."

Randy realized that the very survival of his company was in peril. He turned to government process experts like Baker and Lopez, along with his brother, and two sons working at the company, Wesley and Dalton, to steer EME back in the right direction and regain the needed certification. "Losing Nadcap approval transformed us from a mom and pop business to a real corporate enterprise. In the long run, it forced a necessary business transformation. It was very humbling and surprising the way it worked out," Wesley said. The company estimates that it lost nearly one million dollars that year.

Finally after months of extremely intense work, the industry inspectors returned and EME regained the needed certification in the fall of 2007. "Before we lost our certification there wasn't much structure here, there was a lot more when we got it back and it really helped us as a company," said Baker. When the work returned, so did the employees, many who had not taken another job in hopes they could return to their long-time home. "They were waiting for us when we got the certification back," Dalton said, about the many familiar faces which returned to the workforce.

Somebody else was waiting on EME as well. "After six months, all the customers were still waiting for us, which demonstrates the faith they had in us," one employee stated. The company's greatest crisis turned into its greatest opportunity for success. "It was really a hard time," Wesley admitted. "But in those tough times it proved the company was built to last." The Turnbows and EME had withstood the trials and proved that difficult times transform good into best.

CHAPTER 6

Passing the Torch

Randy Turnbow had pursued a dream of owning a company. His father, Lee, had chosen to walk up the company driveway in order to work for his son. And Steve, while looking for a permanent job, had volunteered to work at EME "temporarily". All three Turnbow men had chosen to work at the company on their own, but Randy never wanted to force his children to follow in their footsteps. In fact, Randy felt all his kids should choose their own path, away from the company. For some of his children, however, their own paths ended up leading *toward* working at EME. "Dad didn't want us to get into the business, but each of us thinks the world of him and regards him as one of our top mentors. It was hard to stay away," Wesley said.

In 1996, Randy's middle son, Dalton, was the first to come to see his father about a permanent job. "My middle son, Matthew Dalton Turnbow—we call him Dalton, expressed to me that he had felt all his life that he would work for me at my company someday," Randy recalled. That day had come for Dalton to follow the same path as his father; to begin his career in the aerospace industry. "I started full time in 1996, as a mag (magnetic) inspector, just like my dad when he started in this business," he said. "I did packing, racking up parts for the line, or whatever it took to show the company I wanted to help it be successful."

Randy appreciated not only his skill, but also his drive. The path Dalton had chosen was leading him to become the third generation of full-time Turnbow employees at EME. "He got training in the aerospace world as a certified magnetic and penetrant inspector," Randy said. "These are the people that look for cracks in the parts that would be unseen by the naked eye, but could lead to disaster if they failed mid-flight on an airplane. I had also entered the industry as an inspector myself and knew that EME was constantly looking for new and reliable inspectors. Dalton fit the bill and was hired. He never looked back."

"Dalton quickly moved up the ladder taking over purchasing and re-organized that area better than it had ever been before," Randy said. "His natural affinity for computers has led him to doing most of the detailed work of keeping track of employees, their training, current work areas, and everything else that has to do with their status within the company." The next generation of full-time Turnbow men proved to be as good a fit for EME as the original three. This knit the family together even tighter.

Dalton discovered that the company functioned smoothly because his family worked so well together. "It's extremely special to work with family," he said. "It's wonderful to see them every day. I know some families don't even get along. I think it's a real blessing."

As Dalton continued to work at EME, he slowly took over more responsibilities, much to the delight of his proud father and uncle. "Dalton has been involved with quality control and taken over the management of the customer service representatives. These folks are vital to the company because they interface with our customers all day long; promising, pushing, and delivering jobs for their specific accounts," Randy said. "We currently do work for nearly 200 accounts and have about 450 customer orders in process at any given time. Again, Dalton had unique talents he brought to the company, and he is currently the "General Manager" of EME.

Dalton, while aware of the challenge, was grateful for the

opportunity to help on a daily basis. "It's a hard industry, and my dad and my uncle Steve do it very well. Sometimes it can be overwhelming to keep up with, but I always look forward to working with them. They have been nothing but supportive of me since I have been here as general manager. I love being out on the floor, making sure we are creating quality product all the time."

Just three years later, another part-time Turnbow became a full-time help, Randy's oldest son, Wesley. He had worked many summers during high school and college, first in maintenance and then in bookkeeping. After graduating with a degree in business administration, Wesley continued at USC in order to pursue law. Then, after receiving his CPA certification through UCLA, he settled into a profitable career as an auditor for Price Waterhouse.

"I was working some sixty hours a week when my wife and I had our first child. This drove me to ask my favorite audit partner, 'How do you jungle your partner responsibilities with your family?' The answer did not encourage me to stick with public accounting." According to the Price Waterhouse partner, the work hours would only increase. He then proceeded to tell a story about working on his laptop during his son's baseball game. This was not the lifestyle Wesley wanted. He wanted to be all-there for his children.

"After five years as an auditor, I knew I needed to make a change for my family's sake; to achieve greater flexibility in my work schedule and to put in fewer hours." That opportunity for change came in a timely manner. Just as Wesley had to choose whether or not to continue a career in public accounting, a job for an accountant opened up at EME.

In 1999, long-time EME bookkeeper, Barbara Graybehl, was retiring after working at EME for 17 years and moving to Arizona. Wesley thought that this opportunity to work with his family would be a perfect fit. He was qualified for the position, but Randy thought maybe he was over-qualified, and did not want him to waste his experience. "I felt like this was not a good use of his talent and schooling, but he convinced me, as he usually does, to let him try working at EME."

"I remember talking in my father's living room one evening. I was done with the big accounting firm career and he was worried about finding a new controller," Wesley relayed. "He told me what a controller made at a small processing company and I told him what an accounting firm paid senior CPA's. We both were silent for a while from the surprise." Eventually, a company vehicle and the promise of flexibility would help bridge this gap.

"I worked with my dad's bookkeeper for six months before she retired," Wesley said. "She taught me payroll and payroll taxes from scratch, and really got me up to speed. I didn't really know metal finishing or manufacturing, but I knew the accounting business and was good at it." Like the rest of the Turnbow men, Wesley was able to put his individual talents to work where he could do the most good for the family and the company.

"With both a law degree from USC and a CPA license, Wesley fit the bill; almost too well," Randy said, after changing his mind about his oldest son returning to the company, first as the controller and then as CEO. Wesley's talent with numbers and his experience as an accountant was sorely needed at EME. "Since I never liked being involved with numbers or accounting, that area failed to keep up with the modern world. Wesley changed all of that forever. He soon brought state-of-the-art financial expertise to EME and ushered us into the modern age of computers," Randy said. This financial upgrade for EME allowed the company to survive the economic crisis soon to arrive.

When a severe depression hit the aerospace industry just months after Wesley took the full-time job, the two young brothers teamed with their father and uncle to weather the storm. "We went into a recession cycle just after he (Wesley) started working here, with very little growth or profit taking place, but his energy and vision for the company were a great boon for EME," Randy said. Like Lee, Randy, and Steve had done in an earlier era, the two young Turnbows remained unified, even during tough times. "Dalton and Wes are always pulling together," Steve said. "It's everything to be together as a family, and it gives us a lot of security."

"We all take responsibility to make sure it's a team effort." After a few years, the industry did gradually begin another financial ascent, and the hard times which the young Turnbows faced had strengthened the mutual bond that brotherhood had initially formed. They had become a cohesive team, ready to further EME's success together.

The youngest son of Randy and Brenda, John Travis, chose not to work at EME full-time, but he has certainly put much effort into the success of the company by working for several summers at EME with quality management and human resources. Because of his gift for languages, Travis was able to translate many necessary employee documents into Spanish, including the current employee handbook. He also helped EME communicate with Airbus in French, which led to them becoming a customer. Travis later moved to Southern France, where he went to work for Airbus, an aircraft manufacturing company. He now works in Paris as a director at Talent Management for Northgate Arinso, an international human resources consulting firm.

"It's an incredible blessing to see the entire family working together," Travis said. "It's pretty wild when you think about all the ups and downs we have been through as a company. Everybody in the family is likable. We are all connected emotionally through the company and with each other." Travis, who studied for his degree at Chapman University and then earned an MBA in France at Toulouse University, gets to return home about once a year and always makes a trip to the ever-growing facility to see its progress. He received his doctorate at Toulouse University in 2012.

"My dad didn't just build some random buildings. He built a

company and a legacy which will stand. Everybody at EME has really stepped up their commitment, and I see the stature of my two brothers grow every time I am there. It's more obvious every time I go back. The one thing that doesn't change is the people. It's very interesting, but they are always the same." While Randy has encouraged each of his kids to follow their own paths, he can't help but miss his youngest, whose path has led him so far away.

"Who knows what the future holds? Maybe he will be back to work one day alongside his brothers. He certainly has a few of the Turnbow aerospace genes in his blood, and a doctorate in human resources sure wouldn't hurt."

In 2007, in the midst of another economic downturn, Randy and Brenda had to institute their next plan to continue the Turnbow and EME family success for future generations. Because of the economic climate and certain tax laws, Randy and Brenda decided to "gift" the company to Wesley and Dalton. Wesley became the CEO and Dalton the General Manager, both now half-owners of the family aerospace business. Randy continued as the board chairman.

"It's something I'm very proud of as a father," Randy said. "When I came up with this idea with my accountant, he said, to me, 'Everybody talks about doing something like this, but they never find the right time to do it. You're one of the few to actually pull the trigger.' I'm glad we did. It was the right thing to do. It looks like we are in good hands, as the company has made record profits since this transfer."

Dalton said he was initially amazed and is now grateful that his father would work so hard to keep EME in the Turnbow family. "It was an amazing thing for dad to do and shows how much he wanted to keep it in the family." Today, Wesley and Randy's desks sit side by side in one office at EME and Dalton is just one room over, with Steve and Jim Baker. The leadership transition went smoothly, as expected. Wesley and Dalton are the official owners of EME, but Randy still comes every day to consult and inspect, and Steve is still working harder than ever to keep up the quality of EME's work.

"Even though it's my company now as the CEO, it would be ridiculous for me to think I knew all I needed to run it. I covet very much the advice of my dad and Uncle Steve. They have so much more experience. If my dad didn't think I should do something, I wouldn't," Wesley said. "There is nothing my dad or Steve hasn't experienced in their decades here. I will come up with this or that idea that I think is new, and my dad will say, 'This is what happened when we did that 15 years ago.'"

"For our family, it's a nice balance," Dalton added. "I want to try and keep it pleasant and keep encouragement in the company. We know our employees have other places to go, and sometimes they do go, but I think most people think of EME as a family and we want to keep it as a family."

With the past success behind them, the present secure, and the future ever-uncertain in a volatile industry, there is only one thing for the EME-Turnbow family to do: continue to reinforce the foundation they have laid for a remarkable future.

CHAPTER 7

Trusting God for the Future

As the Turnbow-EME family gets ready for its second half-century of service to customers, employees, and friends in Southern California and around the world, the future is always uncertain, but the foundation is strong. Sadly, Lee, the original patriarch, passed away in 1998, but Randy, now age 66, has continued his role as inspiration and big-picture leadership. As chairman of EME, he still goes into the office every day and almost always conducts his 8:30 a.m. walk of inspection. "I walk around about the same time every morning to make sure everything is running smoothly and looks good. It definitely seems to help with production and employee relations," Randy said.

It is during these walks that Randy is convinced he is in exactly the right place, at the right company, doing the right thing, because he hasn't lost his passion for both EME and its people. "You know what? This is still fun to me. I love it, and I've loved it since I was a kid. It's not about producing 5,000 widgets every day. It's about helping customers out, each with a job that is special and important to them," he said. While on these daily walks, he sees many familiar faces related by blood or years of hard work and service, and even though EME has gone through so many changes, it still feels like a family.

As a kid, John Travis, now 29, said he witnessed the hard work that goes into the birth and growth of a company, and is now watching his father reap the rich rewards. "It's always been a source of pride and security within the family. My dad is living the American Dream. He was brought up with little, but has been an inspiration to many along the way because of where he has come from." The company he bought for $4,000 in early 1972—worth far less than the purchase price—has become the profitable and performing unit of today. It takes constant renovation, cutting-edge research, dedicated employees, a focus on doing God's work, and dependence on one another to accomplish this. "When I look at where we are now, I know we've come a million miles in progress from where we used to be," said John Lopez, Sr.

Part of the progress at EME is due to the company's new ability to handle an increase in work orders, which continue to flood onto the premises. The NADCAP shut-down really offered EME the opportunity to update its facility, streamline production, and become even more competitive in this now technologically-advanced industry. "January 2012 was a huge month for us, one of the biggest ever," Randy said. "October is usually the biggest month because everybody wants to get their project done by the end of the year."

Progress also comes from the never-ending quest for the latest techniques in order to make the company even more competitive. "As recently as 2009 I set out on a mission to discover how to perform anodize on titanium for military aircraft," said Randy. "After months of searching, I discovered a secret formula in a little known part of near-eastern Europe. Today we have the largest titanium anodizing line in America that is approved by Lockheed for the new F-35 program, which is the largest military contract in history."

Working with longtime, dedicated employees, has enabled EME to progress as well, according to Randy, who named a few key contributors. "In those years a man named Frank Anguiano showed up as a maintenance man and he could do everything from welding, boiler work and construction, to electrical design. He and his brother, Porfirio Anguiano, have literally built EME from the ground up and are still working hard here today. Another key employee is Ricardo Osorio, who has worked for EME most of his life and in the last few years has filled a vital role as a link between quality control and the actual chemical processing of the parts. He is now the "Operations Manager". Frank has a younger brother, Jesus Silva, who came to work with us for many years and he was very bright and had a heart for the growth and success of EME.

"Men like John Lopez Jr., Ricardo Osorio, Steve Robbins, and many more are the true future of EME. And with these dedicated employees, I must say the future looks bright. EME's quality is famous, and it is in some measure, because the final inspection of the parts by Gabriel Ibarra. He has done a great job of this for a number of years. In the same way, Joe Lipsey has run our critical penetrant department better than anyone ever has in our history." With such talent and dedication as the backbone of the "family", there isn't much that will be able to slow EME down for too long; not even an ownership transfer.

Wesley said that the manner in which the transfer of the company was handled and accepted has been of great importance to the future success of EME. The smooth transfer of ownership depicted the immense dedication and humility present in the company, which is so vital to achieving and maintaining a unified body. Wesley was really touched by his Uncle Steve's response to him inheriting EME. "When my dad gifted the company to us, my Uncle Steve said, 'I'm ready to work for you boss.' That meant a lot. I love that we can change things around with this family. And when you do it the right way, it helps the employees, and it helps the family." This dedication and unity creates an environment that people want to be a part of. "My uncle wants to work here until he dies. My dad wants to continue to enjoy the company that he built. He still takes charge of pricing, which is very difficult, and handles a lot of customer relations because he knows everybody."

Randy said that despite his long tenure at the company, his sons are coming up with new and better ideas, especially for things which matter most and will stand for eternity. One goal of the new ownership team is to permeate their working environment with their faith in God. "Another gift that Dalton and Wesley brought to the company was a true Christian caring for the employees' welfare and this has begun to affect me as well. In 1999, I was compelled to join a Christian businessmen's group called FCCI (Fellowship of Companies for Christ International). I had always counted myself as a Christian, and they taught the concept that a Christian's company was really just another gift from God. Therefore, my role as owner should be as caretaker of 'God's company'. The concept was to run my company using Biblical principles. As I began to practice these goals, I found myself caring more for my employees and doing the honorable thing in business, no matter the costs."

One change that is attributed to being a part of FCCI has been the implementation of the Marketplace Chaplains in his company. In 2005 Randy and Brenda attended an FCCI conference and became acquainted with a man named Gil Stricklin, and the company he founded, Marketplace Ministries. "I discovered that companies all over most of the United States used this private company to supply chaplains for their company or corporation." After further research, Randy decided to have this service available to his employees, thus making EME the first company in California to use the Dallas-based chaplain service.

Immediately, Randy began to see how advantageous it was having a chaplain on the premises of EME. He became more aware of the employees' problems and was able to provide empathy and support. "The chaplains would walk through our company and chat briefly and privately with any employee who wished to talk with them about the problems of life they were encountering. This counseling would cover anything from spiritual and emotional problems they were having, to problems with their family or their children. The conversation was often about an illness, injury or death in the family, a job loss, or legal problems. These types of situations, I soon discovered, affected all employees and also affected their work potential because of worry and time away from the company. I quickly realized that no safety net existed for these types of problems for our people, and I had to do something about it."

Employees of companies who hire chaplains benefit greatly from the services provided to them free of charge. Besides free counseling and spiritual guidance, the hired chaplain was available to perform employee weddings and preside over funerals at zero cost to them. This saves EME employees a large amount of money, provides more peace of mind, and helps them make wise decisions. It has been a huge success.

"We have now had chaplains for seven years and the concept has spread like wildfire all over California. I smile and tell Gil Stricklin that someday California will have more Chaplains than any other state. I pray I'm right because my employees love the chaplain service." Providing spiritual guidance and services to employees has been another step to securing future success the right way.

The management team also intends to maintain a thriving business by continuing to use their strengths to better EME, and working to keep relationships strong. Dalton, 34, said that regardless of what the future holds, they will continue to depend on each others' expertise for success. "I don't think I could do this without Wesley and his skill with numbers. It's a great thing that we work so well together. We complement each other. I don't even have to think about the money because Wesley handles that, and I work with the employees."

"When we kick around ideas with Randy and Steve and John that relate to the company, you just can't go wrong with all of that experience," said Wesley, 43. "My brother was the best man in my wedding, and we are still great friends. We work well together, and always have each others' back. Dad and I are very even keel while Dalton and Steve are more emotional. Each demeanor has its strengths and weaknesses. We are able to keep each other in balance."

"I'm really glad God allowed the Turnbows to work together with all our different strengths. Everybody in the family has worked here, either full-time, part-time, or by giving us the support we need at home. We all have a different skill set, which keeps everybody interdependent and connected," Randy said. "Dalton is popular with the employees and loves managing them. Steve is a genius with chemicals and concepts. I'm good with logistics and big concepts. Wesley is all about numbers, administration, and details. My dad, Lee was a tremendous designer. We are all able to get our jobs done without stepping on each other's toes."

RANDY LEADS TROOPS IN MORNING EXERCISES "JUST 50 MORE"

Randy, who has been a part of EME's progress more than anyone alive, said he is grateful for a reason to celebrate an anniversary milestone and looks forward to many more in the future. Don't even mention retirement around the Turnbows, the word means nothing to them. Instead, Randy and Steve are taking the opportunity to focus on preparing the next generation of leaders. "Steve and I both still work hard, but we enjoy mentoring a whole level of the younger generation which we know will make us proud—because we trained them," Randy said.

With all the pieces in place, the Turnbows and their dedicated employees are ready, willing and able to help EME's future be as brilliant as a Southern California sunrise, and now for a higher purpose. "I have a sense of helping others out, whether they are our employees or the nonprofit organizations we give to," Wesley said. "I'm pleased with where the future is leading us. It's a very exciting time, a very exciting future."

"We always knew we would have fun," said Brenda. But she never dreamed it would be such a successful adventure when she entered the Turnbow family so long ago. It has fulfilled their long-standing desire to make things better for themselves and for those to come. "It was all about making the family better generation by generation." Thus the Turnbow family will continue adding more love, more strength, more unshakeable faith in God and family, to the fifty-year foundation it has laid, hoping to see many more decades to come.

Turnbow Biographies

Randall (Randy) Turnbow

I was born to Lee and Evelyne on January 21, 1946. At a young age I loved to build model airplanes. I went Lakewood High school, was on a championship basketball team and on the track team as a shot-putter. After graduating I attended Cal State University at Long Beach.

My goal as a young man was to own my own company after I had worked summers in a metal finishing company. That first company was California Metal Processing where I became the General Manager.

I went to NDT trade school at Magnaflux Corp. to learn Magnetic and Penetrant Inspection. Later I learned X-ray and Ultrasonic Inspection while working at General Inspection Laboratories after I got out of Basic Training at Fort Ord, California.

I started a NDT consultant company and completely put together all the equipment training material and QC manual regarding Mag and Penetrant Inspection for a company called Watkin's Deburring.

Later I became part owner in Alert Metal Finishing which did Hard-Chrome and Cadmium Plating. I also was buying for a short time AAA Inspection Labs and Plating just before I bought EME.

I married on September 17, 1965 to Brenda K Harris. I got involved in my church and participated in many roles. Our first child was Rhanda whom was born on February 20, 1967. Two years later Wesley Steven was born on February 28, 1969, then Matthew Dalton on November 23, 1977, and John Travis on August 1, 1982.

In 1999 I joined an international Christian Fellowship composed of company CEO's. This group called FCCI changed my life and the way I looked at my business more than anything in my life. I began to see my business as God's company, in which I was to be the steward thereof. Through this group I discovered Marketplace Chaplains Company which I hired to work at EME; which also was a tremendous change for both me and my employees.

RANDY AND STEVE WITH AIRPLANES

RANDY AND BRENDA

RANDY AND STEVE WITH
CHAPLAIN WES SULLIVAN

Steve Turnbow

Son of Lee and Evelyne Turnbow on March 28, 1949. My family was interesting with regard to formal religion. My grandparents on my mother's side were Catholic but she regularly attended the local Christian church. My Dad and his side of the family was for the most part Mormon. When I was about twelve years old my mother asked me if I wanted to be baptized. Having been attending Catholic, Christian, and Mormon churches, at that time, I elected not to be baptized.

His education was at Holmes Elementary School through 6th grade, Hoover Jr. High 7th through 9th grade, Lakewood High School 10th through 12th. After, he attended Long Beach City College Technology Campus for two years, then to Northrop University for three years. He got FAA certified Airframe and Powerplants, ASTN NDT Level 3 Certified Turbine Engine Mechanic, and Certified Airframe Electrician.

He was married to Melody E. Agal in the 1970's and three years later had a son, Bryan J. Turnbow.

About 1985 I began to hear the sound of Jesus knocking at my door and within a few months I quietly accepted the Lord. I thought it might be a good thing if I were to be baptized so I contacted several local churches. In all cases the answer was no because I had to join the congregation and receive suit able training prior to baptism. I explained that I just wanted to go to the river, meet John the Baptist, and be born again. My request was declined, so I went about my duties.

One night after I was leaving my second shift, I was listening to a radio minister named Gene Scott. I recall he said that on the next Sunday morning, he was going to have a stampede baptism. The event was scheduled to baptize any person who showed up. On that Sunday morning hundreds of people showed up, including me. In the parking lot four large portable swimming pools were filled at the waist deep. The area appeared to be an abandoned industrial section of the city of Los Angeles. There was no traffic or other people in the area. There were abandoned buildings all around, there were no sounds, and hundreds of people stood quietly. At seven in the morning five people began taking their places in each pool to begin praying and baptizing those who were willing. No church, no questions asked, I was born again.

BUILDING EME

STEVE AND MELODY

Lee Turnbow

Lee Turnbow was born October 18, 1919, to Eva and Paul Turnbow, in Utah. He seldom spoke about his childhood and preferred to keep his personal life private. His lifelong hobby was to make and draw-up inventions and to make improvements on everyday products. He attended school, finishing at Roosevelt High School in Roosevelt, Utah. After graduation he traveled to California to inquire about employment. Lee worked in the dry-cleaning industry, then as a machinist in the aerospace industry, was a well-known salesman, and an engineer in the metal finishing industry.

His goal was and is to have a strong, loving family. Evelyne Elaine Kinikin, was born to George and Anna Kinikin on March 7th, 1924 in Garden City, Kansas. Since she was young she was passionate in singing and dancing. At 15 her family and she moved to California, she met Lee, and later married him on June 7th 1944. Two years later, a son, Randall, was born and two years later another son, Steven, was born.

In 1994 Lee and Evelyne celebrated their 50th anniversary. After they celebrated three more years together, Lee passed away on January 19, 1998.

This year, 2012 at eighty-eight years young Evelyne is still singing, choreographing, and playing the hand bells, being not only a member but also the author of the original charter for the California's Women's Chorus.

Wesley Turnbow

I was born at the Long Beach Memorial Hospital on February 28, 1969 to Randy and Brenda Turnbow. I was the second child and the first boy. I have been told that my dad was beside himself to have a little red-headed baby. I grew up mostly in Long Beach, CA with a love for model trains, making people laugh, and singing. I started playing soccer in elementary school and continued to play into my 40's. Each year for my birthday weekend I took a close friend to my grandparents', Lee & Evelyne's house, in Ojai, a boy's paradise!

I graduated from Brethren High School in 1987. Then he attended University of Southern California, gaining a degree in business finance (1991) and a juris doctor degree (1994). I met my wife at Southland Christian Church in Bell Gardens, CA where I was attracted to her faith, her beauty, and her singing voice. Michelle and I were married on February 5, 1994 at Wilmington First Christian Church. I worked my way through for the Los Angeles County District Attorney then for 5 years as an auditor for Price Waterhouse. My wife and I had our first child, Abigail on January 9, 1999. My father and I came to an employment agreement in March of 1999 I was hired as

the controller at E.M.E. After, my wife and I began alternating having baby boys and girls over the next 12 years of our marriage. LUKE RANDALL (6/18/2001), EVELYNE (11/14/2003), JOHN WESLEY (6/9/2005), REBECCA (4/10/2008), AND JOSEPH (8/28/2010).

Dalton Turnbow

Dalton Turnbow was born to Randy and Brenda Turnbow on November 23, 1977 in Long Beach, California. Dalton enjoyed sports including; soccer, baseball, surfing and football.

Dalton graduated from Valley Christian High School in Cerritos California in 1996. After he worked at EME as a non-destructive testing inspector, purchasing manager, and the operations manager prior to becoming the general manager. He has had continuous Nadcap training including; Chemical Processing, Non-Destructive Testing, Aerospace Contract Review, Root Cause and Corrective Action, Internal Auditing, ITAR/EAR and Pyrometry.

Steven M. Robbins was and is still his best friend. Steven has worked at EME from 1999 to the present. He is currently the Laboratory Supervisor.

He married his childhood sweetheart, Rebecca D. Lowell, in 2004. They attended sixth grade together, were very close, but they did not reunite after that until just after high school. In 2012 they were blessed with a baby boy, Wyatt.

Bryan J. Turnbow

Bryan was born April 12th, 1973 and is the only child of Steven and Melody Turnbow. Most of his weekends were spent enjoying the outdoors, skiing, surfing, and camping.

Bryan went to Millikan High School and graduated from Chapman University with a Bachelor's degree in Business and Communications. Out of college he started a small business at Fred Segal in Santa Monica. After a few years he moved on to finance, became licensed, and started his career at Prudential Securities. From there he moved on to Fisher Investments out of Woodside, CA. Since 2005 he has been with Churchill Management Group where he serves as a regional Vice-President for Orange and San Diego counties.

Bryan married Summer in Santa Barbara, CA on April 28th, 2001. Summer and Bryan met when they were twelve years old at Marshall Junior High and as they say, "the rest is history". They are the proud parents of Noah Daniel, born on February 24th, 2005. Following in the footsteps of their parents, the family can often be found at the beach or enjoying the mountains and lake of Big Bear, CA.

Bryan always believed in God and cannot remember a time when he did not. More recently, with the loving support of Summer and Noah, they have strengthened their faith and growing together in Christ.

Through his family's dedication and hard work, EME Inc. has defied the odds, thrived and grown and taken care of our entire family. God Bless EME!

John Travis Turnbow

Travis was born and raised in Long Beach, California to Randall and Brenda Turnbow on August 1, 1982. As a child he loved art and music. He competed at the state level for piano and often filled the living room with sound, for better or for worse, as he worked through a new sheet of music. He also played other instruments and actively participated in marching band, jazz, and orchestral youth ensembles. Travis was also an Eagle Scout, an honor that he owes to his father who served as a scout leader for years.

Travis graduated from Valley Christian High School in 2000 and then from Chapman University in 2004 where he majored in French and Spanish. After his undergraduate studies, Travis' love of language and culture led him to Puerto Rico and then to Southern France where he worked as a translator and taught Basic English. A true Francophile, once in France, he never really left. Upon obtaining an MBA from the University of Toulouse in 2007, Travis began his career in international human resources and workforce planning at Airbus. He is currently the Head of Talent Management at the Paris site of NorthgateArinso, an HR consulting firm. Although Travis endeavors to move forward in his career, work has never been his first priority and he considers that he works to live and does not live to work.

Growing up in a Christian family, Travis gave his life to God as a young boy. However, it was not until later on that he began to understand the implications of this decision. Today, he is continually surprised by the mercifulness of God as a Friend. Travis remarks that this relationship has changed him forever. The same God that makes one man's life worth living brings meaning to the story of all men.

EME Employees and Their Years of Service

30 YEARS AND OVER

Steve Turnbow 37 years
Juan Chavez 32 years
Daniel Munguia 31 years

Guillermo Diaz 30 years
John Lopez Sr. 30 years
Elias Avila 30 years

OVER 20 YEARS

Manuel Gaxiola 27 years
Maria Garcia 25 years
Simon Quiroz 25 years
Jesus Marquez 24 years
Eudulia Guizar 23 years

Cresencio Galindo 23 years
Ricardo Esquivel 22 years
Ricardo Alcazar 21 years
Frank Anguiano 21 years

OVER 15 YEARS

Jose Sigaran 18 years
Alfredo Garcia 18 years
Joe Lipsey 18 years
Porfirio Anguiano 17 years
Yvonne Garcia 17 years
Rogelio Murillo 17 years
Pedro Naranjo 17 years
Frank Rivera 17 years
Eloy Sandoval 17 years

Esperanza Ramirez 16 years
Miguel Osorio 16 years
Arturo Rojas 16 years
Juan Guzman 16 years
Roberto Alfaro 16 years
Saul Melendez16 years
James Baker 15 years
Gabriel Ibarra 15 years

CPSIA information can be obtained at www.ICGtesting.com
Printed in the USA
LVIW01n2036051116
511593LV00003B/3